A science
The Magic School Bus®
CHAPTER BOOK

THE SEARCH
for the
MISSING BONES

SCHOLASTIC INC.
New York   Toronto   London   Auckland   Sydney
Mexico City   New Delhi   Hong Kong   Buenos Aires

Written by Eva Moore.

Illustrations by Ted Enik.

Based on *The Magic School Bus* books
written by Joanna Cole and illustrated by Bruce Degen.

The author would like to acknowledge Stephen C. Allen, M.D., for his expert
advice in preparing this manuscript.

ISBN 0-439-10799-7

60 59 58 57 56 55 54 53 52   13 14 15 16/0

Designed by Peter Koblish

Printed in the U.S.A.

INTRODUCTION

My name is Dorothy Ann — D.A. for short. I am one of the kids in Ms. Frizzle's class.

Maybe you have heard of Ms. Frizzle. (Sometimes we just call her the Friz.) She is a terrific teacher — but strange. Her favorite subject is science, and she knows *everything*.

She takes us on lots of field trips in the Magic School Bus. Believe me, it's not called *magic* for nothing!

We never know what's going to happen when we get on that bus.

Ms. Frizzle likes to surprise us, but we can usually tell when she is planning a special lesson — we just look at what she's wearing.

Last Halloween, though, Ms. Frizzle really did surprise us — and she had help from a bunch of ghosts.

Does that sound impossible? Well, let me tell you what happened. . . .

CHAPTER 1

"I'm going to be a vampire," Ralphie said.

"I'm going to be a mermaid," Wanda said.

"I'm going to be a bunch of grapes," Arnold said. "What about you, D.A.?"

"It's a secret," I said. "I want to surprise everybody."

We were talking about our costumes for Halloween. It was just a few days away, and we could hardly wait to get dressed up.

Little did we know that all our plans were about to fly out the window.

The adventure began when Ms. Frizzle walked in wearing a dress with tiny bones all over it. She was carrying a large orange carton. Something long, green, and scaly was stretched out across the box. Nobody was scared. It was only Liz, Ms. Frizzle's pet lizard.

"Good morning, class," the Friz sang out. "As you know, it's nearly Halloween. To celebrate, I thought we could have an early Halloween party this afternoon."

"But we don't have our costumes," Tim said.

"Not to worry, Tim. I have brought special costumes that will get us all in the mood," Ms. Frizzle said. "Plus, these costumes are a perfect fit for our new science unit."

I was curious about the new science unit. (Science is one of my best subjects. I always carry a science notebook so I can write down all the facts I learn.)

I was curious about what was in the box, too. Liz had climbed off, and I could see big black letters across the top.

"Class, we're about to get down to the bare bones!" Ms. Frizzle announced. She opened the box and reached inside.

"As you can see, our new unit will be about . . ."

"Skeletons!" we all called out as she held up the neatest skeleton costume I had ever seen.

"Right you are!" the Friz said. There were more costumes in the box. Ms. Frizzle gave one to each of us. "Without our skeletons, we'd be nothing but blobs. It's time we learned about what keeps us all in shape."

The skeleton costumes were cool. They were full length, with feet. And the bones weren't just painted on, like the costumes you get in a store. They were made of shiny white vinyl material and were stuck onto the front and back of the black bodysuit with Velcro strips. There were separate gloves with hand bones attached.

Ms. Frizzle — being Ms. Frizzle — had gotten a costume for herself and a special lizard skeleton suit for Liz.

We all pulled on the costumes, and soon the room was full of walking, talking, laughing skeletons.

"Hey, Ms. Frizzle," Ralphie said, "there's something wrong with your skeleton. You don't have a backbone!"

"And look at you, Ralphie," Phoebe said. "You don't have hand bones!"

We started walking around looking at one another. There were bones missing from every costume:

Tim didn't have his lower leg bones.

Wanda didn't have foot bones.

Keesha didn't have thighbones.

Carlos looked strange without upper arm bones.

And Arnold was missing shoulder blades and collarbones.

Phoebe's top half looked funny — she didn't seem to have any ribs.

And when I looked at my forearms, they weren't there. There was nothing between my elbows and my hands.

Ms. Frizzle was standing next to a chart of the human skeleton she had just put up.

"Hmmmm," she said. "I think Hugh Mann's Costume Company has some explaining to do. Our costumes should all look something like our friend Skinny here. As soon as we finish today's lesson, I think we'll take a little ride to the costume company and find out what happened."

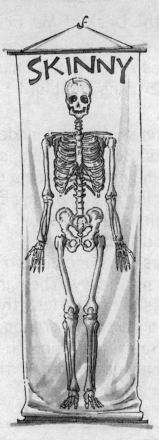

We learned some amazing facts about the bones of the human skeleton that afternoon.

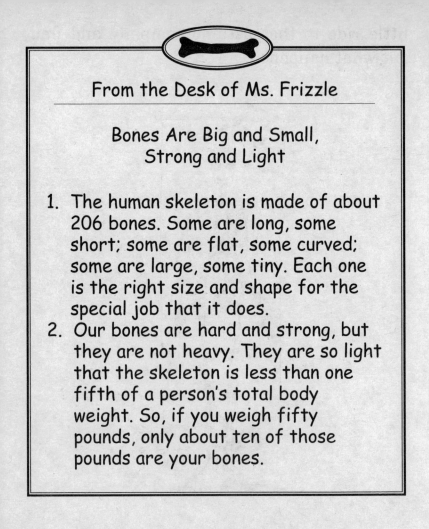

From the Desk of Ms. Frizzle

Bones Are Big and Small, Strong and Light

1. The human skeleton is made of about 206 bones. Some are long, some short; some are flat, some curved; some are large, some tiny. Each one is the right size and shape for the special job that it does.
2. Our bones are hard and strong, but they are not heavy. They are so light that the skeleton is less than one fifth of a person's total body weight. So, if you weigh fifty pounds, only about ten of those pounds are your bones.

Then Ms. Frizzle grabbed her keys.

"Okay, everybody," she announced, "to the bus!"

We all piled into the Magic School Bus. The bus had taken us on many wacky adventures, and somehow we knew this trip would not be an ordinary ride.

"Where is Hugh Mann's Costume Company?" Arnold asked.

"Oh," the Friz answered, "it's just a quick flight to Skeleton City."

Skeleton City?

Liz sat up front with the Friz as she turned on the ignition. Before we left the school parking lot, the bus had transformed into the Magic School Jet. We were off!

CHAPTER 2

The Magic School Jet zoomed through the blue sky. We were all still thinking about Skeleton City when Ms. Frizzle switched on the automatic pilot and took out her harmonica.

"We need a rousing song," she said. "How about 'The Ghost of John'? Let's sing it as a round. Hit it!"

Tim began, and we each followed in turn:

"Have you seen the ghost of John?
Long white bones and the rest all gone.

Oo, oo, oo, oo, oo, oo, oo, oo,
Wouldn't it be chilly with no skin on?"

The Magic School Jet landed just as we finished the round, and the jet changed back to a bus.

From the parking lot, we took a good look at the costume company. It looked like a spooky old castle.

As we followed Ms. Frizzle into the main

office, something started to howl! Nobody at the factory seemed to notice the freaky howls except for us. Whatever it was, it howled ten times and then stopped.

All the factory employees just kept working. People were rushing around, pushing carts piled high with cartons or waving papers madly.

Phones were buzzing. . . .

A skinny man with wild hair burst out of a door marked:

HUGH D. MANN
PRESIDENT AND CEO

"Who took this order for five hundred Dracula costumes?" he demanded. "We'll never be able to get that many fangs in time."

"Sorry, sir," a young woman said. "I forgot to tell you about the order. Don't worry; I'll take care of it." She hurried off.

Mr. Mann jumped when he saw us standing there in our bones.

"Who are you?" he asked.

"I'm Ms. Frizzle, and these are my students," the Friz told him. "We have a bone to pick with you. There's something wrong with all our costumes — as you can see. We want new ones, with the proper number of bones."

Hugh Mann looked as if he were about to cry. "Oh, dear," he said. "I guess the workers tried to rush your order out and got a little careless. We've been so busy with Halloween right around the corner. And, I'm sorry to say, we are completely sold out of our deluxe skeleton costumes."

He thought for a minute. "I can't spare any workers to fix your costumes right now, but I have an idea. There are a lot of extra bones in the stockrooms. Would you mind searching for the missing bones yourselves? I'll show you the way."

Mr. Mann took us outside and pointed to a barnlike building. "That's where you start, Ms. Frizzle — Stockroom A," he said. "Ah, I see you have a bus. Good. You can drive right onto the conveyor belt. It will take you

through all the bone stockrooms. Use this remote to stop and start the belt."

Then Mr. Mann reached into his pocket and pulled out a piece of paper.

"Here's a map of the buildings you'll be going through. You can stop wherever you like and pick up your missing bones."

Ms. Frizzle barely got out a thank-you before Mr. Mann disappeared into the busy office.

A couple of minutes later we were back in the bus. Ms. Frizzle drove onto a wide band of rubber, like the belts that carry luggage in an airport. She turned off the engine and pushed the *go* button on the remote. The conveyor belt started with a whir. We were all nervous that the spooky howls would start again.

We glided along into a huge room with a large letter *A* above the door. Ms. Frizzle pushed the *stop* button on the remote.

"Class, get ready to begin the great bone search," she said. "We need to hurry to get back for the Halloween party. So let's go. The map says that Stockroom A is the place for feet. Now we just have to find a pair that fits Wanda."

There were boxes stacked on shelves and on the floor — each one full of bones.

"How are we ever going to find the right ones for my costume?" Wanda moaned. "There are so many different sizes."

Ms. Frizzle gave us a pep talk. "As my great-great-great-granduncle Phineas Finder used to say, 'With lots of eyes, you'll find the prize.'"

Some of us paired up. Phoebe and I tore into one box while Ralphie and Carlos attacked another. Liz gave Ms. Frizzle a hand.

"What if we can't find the right size feet to fit Wanda?" Keesha worried.

"We *have* to. We need to get back for Ms. Frizzle's party," Phoebe said.

"Bingo!" we heard Tim yell. "I think I found the right pair of feet for Wanda." He bent down and pressed the vinyl foot bones onto the Velcro strips on Wanda's costume.

A perfect fit.

"Boy, feet are really bony," said Wanda, looking at the new additions to her costume.

"That's the truth," Ms. Frizzle said. "Each foot has twenty-six bones."

"I'll remember that for my report," Wanda said.

Bony Feet
by Wanda

Just think! Feet have 52 of the 206 bones in your body! That's more than any other part of the skeleton except the hands.

Foot bones are flatter and longer than hand bones.

The shape of the foot helps to keep us from falling forward when we stand.

Tibia

Fibula

Tarsals

Achille's Tendon

Phalanges

Metatarsals

Talus (anklebone)

Take a Walk
by Wanda

Have you ever noticed how your feet can change shape and bend as you walk? Feet are very flexible because they are made of so many bones. The shape of our feet helps us walk on different kinds of surfaces.

CHAPTER 3

As we were climbing back into the bus, we heard the spooky howl again. "Wh-what was th-that?" Arnold asked.

Whatever it was, it kept howling until it had howled eleven times! We were too scared to move. Then the howls stopped, and everything was silent. We all took our seats in the bus without saying a word.

Ms. Frizzle checked the map Mr. Mann had given her. "Next is Stockroom B," she said, "leg bones!" She pushed the button on the remote that started the conveyor belt moving.

Wanda was wiggling her new feet. "Bones are so hard and stiff," she said. "But we can move easily. How come, Ms. Frizzle?"

"Good question, Wanda!" Ms. Frizzle said. "I have a feeling we'll find the answer when we check out these posters."

As the bus moved slowly along the conveyor belt, she pulled a lever and several posters rolled out of the dashboard.

Our Bones Can Move Because of MUSCLES and JOINTS

MUSCLES Give Us the Power to Move, and They Give Us Strength

Muscles are attached to the bones with stringy "ropes" called TENDONS. The muscles pull on the bones and make them move.

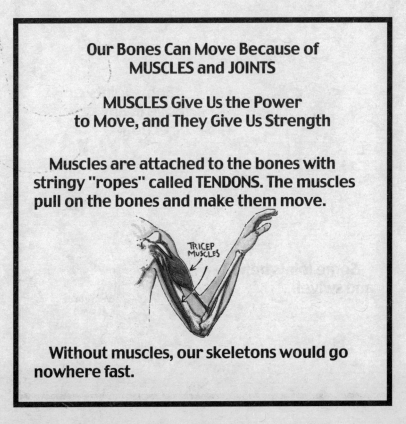

TRICEP MUSCLES

Without muscles, our skeletons would go nowhere fast.

JOINTS Are Places Where Two Bones Meet

Some of our joints only move backward and forward.

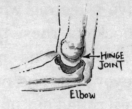

HINGE JOINT

Elbow

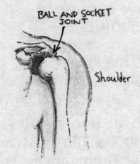

BALL AND SOCKET JOINT

Shoulder

Some joints can move in any direction.

Some joints bend and swivel.

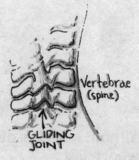

Vertebrae (spine)

GLIDING JOINT

Some turn side to side and rotate.

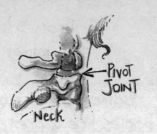

Neck

PIVOT JOINT

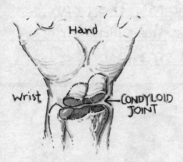

Hand

Wrist

CONDYLOID JOINT

Some joints in the wrist move side to side and back and forth.

Thumb

SADDLE JOINT

The joint at the base of the thumb moves in two directions.

The bones are held in place at the joint with stretchy LIGAMENTS, which are like tough rubber bands.

From D.A.'s Notebook
Human Pretzels

Some people can bend and twist their bodies like a pretzel. We say they are "double-jointed." But they don't really have extra joints. They can bend easily because their ligaments are extra long and stretchy.

By now we had arrived at Stockroom B, where the lower leg bones were stored. Ms. Frizzle turned off the magic monitor and stopped the conveyor belt. We got out of the bus and followed her into the dark room.

"Okay, class," said the Friz, "you may have heard that the leg bone's connected to the ankle bone. But as you will see, each lower leg is actually made of two bones, and the ankle is really just the bottom end of those bones! Now, let's start looking for a pair of lower legs — two bones for each leg — that will fit Tim's costume."

We went through one box of bones after another. Some bones were too long, and some were too short. We were searching so hard that we almost didn't hear the rustling noise in a dark corner. All of a sudden, a box came crashing to the floor!

"Wh-wh-what is that?" Ralphie asked. He was pointing toward the noise. We froze. There in the dark corner was a tall skeleton with glowing green bones. It was looking right at us with its enormous eye sockets.

Then in a blink of an eye — it dis-appeared!

We couldn't move.

"You know what that was?" Ralphie said at last. "That was the ghost of John — long white bones and the rest all gone!"

I admit the skeleton was a scary sight, but I never let my imagination run away with me. "Don't be silly," I said. "There are no such things as ghosts."

"How do you know, D.A.?" Wanda asked. "It looked like a ghost to me — a skeleton ghost!"

Ms. Frizzle went over to the box of spilled bones. "If it was a ghost, I think it must be a helpful sort," she said. "These look like the leg bones we've been searching for."

She attached the bones to Tim's cos-tume.

"Neat," said Tim. "Now I've got it all together!"

"Good," said Arnold. "Now we can get out of here."

One Bone, Two Bones
by Tim

The large shin bone in the front of your leg is called the tibia.

The thinner bone to the outside is the fibula.

For walking and running, you can't have one without the other!

Fibula   Tibia

Back on the bus, Ms. Frizzle checked the map.

"Thighbones coming up," she said. She pushed the remote button, and we moved along the conveyor belt. We were just turning a bend when an eerie glow appeared behind us. We looked out the back window and gasped — there in the dark shadows was the skeleton. The ghost of John was back!

"It's following us!" Phoebe cried.

But the ghost didn't move at all. It just disappeared.

CHAPTER 4

We could hardly wait to get out of the factory. It was really giving us the creeps.

"You might know we'd end up in a haunted factory at Halloween time," Arnold said.

"What did you expect?" said Keesha. "This *is* a Magic School Bus trip."

Tim was walking up and down the aisle of the bus, stretching his legs and admiring his new tibia and fibula.

"These costume bones are made of vinyl," Tim said, "but what about our real bones, Ms. Frizzle? What are they made of?"

"Our bones are made of hard calcium

phosphate and tough, stringy collagen," Ms. Frizzle answered. "A bone seems solid, but let's see what it's really like inside."

The Friz pushed a button on the dashboard. At once, the bus's windshield became a giant TV monitor. A picture flashed on the screen.

"This drawing shows the parts of the thighbone," Ms. Frizzle said. "The thighbone is also called the femur."

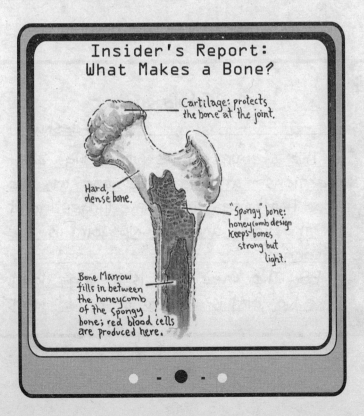

Insider's Report: What Makes a Bone?

Cartilage: protects the bone at the joint.

Hard, dense bone.

"Spongy" bone: honeycomb design keeps bones strong but light.

Bone Marrow fills in between the honeycomb of the spongy bone; red blood cells are produced here.

"Wow!" Ralphie exclaimed. "There's a lot more to our bones than I thought."

"And remember that there are blood vessels inside the bones. There are nerves all around them, too," the Friz said. "That's why we feel pain when a bone gets a hard blow."

Just then Ms. Frizzle stopped the conveyor belt. We were inside Stockroom C.

The bones in this building were marked *long, longer,* and *longest.*

The Fabulous Femur
by Keesha

The femur makes two big connections — at the knee and at the hip. The knee joint is the largest joint in the body, and the hip joint is the strongest.

P.S. The knee joint is a hinge joint. The hip joint is a ball-and-socket joint.

"The femur is the longest bone in the body," Ms. Frizzle told us as we began searching through the boxes. "In fact, it makes up one fourth of a person's height."

I did the math. Keesha is about four feet tall, so we needed to find thighbones about one foot long.

"These two look about right," said Arnold. "Let's see if they fit Keesha."

The knob at the top of each of the femurs fit perfectly into the hip joints of Keesha's costume, and the large knee joints stuck right into place.

Q: Which Joints Wear Caps?
A: Your Knees!
by Arnold

The kneecap is a small, flat bone that protects the sensitive knee joint. It is a separate bone, connected by tendons to the front of the joint.

Hip, Hip, Hooray
by Keesha

   The curved hipbones make a cradle, called the pelvis, that protects the stomach, intestines, and other soft insides. The shape helps to keep our legs in line with the top half of our body so we can keep our balance.

Stomach

intestines

Pelvis

We were so busy connecting Keesha's thighbones that no one noticed the conveyor belt starting up . . . until it was too late.

"Hey, stop!" called Tim. "The bus is heading into the tunnel without us. Someone must have punched the remote."

We ran to the conveyor belt. There up ahead in the bus we could see a strange form in the driver's seat — those ghostly glowing bones again! And looking out the back window were the frightened eyes of a small lizard. Liz was being kidnapped on the bus!

CHAPTER 5

"Quick, everyone — hop onto the conveyor belt," Ms. Frizzle called. "We need to follow that bus!"

The belt wasn't moving very fast, but jumping onto it was tricky. Everyone made it after one try, except Ralphie.

Ralphie jogged along next to the conveyor belt. "I'll never get on!" he cried.

"Yes, you will!" I said. "We'll help you. We'll count to three. Ready? One, two, three."

He hopped up, and we grabbed his arms. He made it! Now we were all riding along on the conveyor belt. We went through a tunnel marked Stockroom D.

"I hope that ghost skeleton knows how to stop this thing," Ralphie said.

We all breathed a sigh of relief when the conveyor belt came to a gentle stop inside the building. We could see the bus at the other end.

Ms. Frizzle hurried to the bus. We stayed safely back, in case the ghost was still there, waiting to spook us.

"All clear!" the Friz called out. "Never fear, no ghosts are here." We ran to the bus and checked out the inside. Everything looked normal.

Liz popped up from behind a seat. When she saw Ms. Frizzle, she jumped into her arms.

"Poor Liz," said Phoebe. "I bet she was really scared. I'm glad she's okay."

"Let's get to work and find some bones," Ms. Frizzle said. "We'll worry about the ghost later." She opened the building map.

"This is the backbone stockroom!" she announced. "Ah, a spine at last is mine."

The shelves in Stockroom D were stacked with long boxes.

"Thank goodness these spines are all put together," Arnold said. "It would take us years to find the right thirty-three vertebrae for Ms. Frizzle."

"Here's one that looks good," Tim called. We held it up to Ms. Frizzle's back.

"All right!" Carlos said. "This spine is fine!"

"S" Is for Spine
by Tim

Maybe you thought your backbone was perfectly straight up and down. Well, it isn't. From a side view, you can see a long, S-shaped curve. The curve helps the spine stay strong, absorbs jolts when we walk and run, and makes the spine more flexible.

From the Desk of Ms. Frizzle

Your Spine Is Made of 33 Bones

The bones of the spine are called vertebrae.

The bones lock into the skull at the top and the pelvis at the bottom to support the whole skeleton.

Count the vertebrae:
Neck — 7 vertebrae
Upper back — 12 vertebrae
Lower back — 5 vertebrae
Sacrum — 5 vertebrae often fused
    together into one bone
Coccyx — 4 vertebrae frequently
    joined to one another
Total number of vertebrae = 33

Vertebrae are linked together by gliding joints. Because of these joints we can arch backward, twist our body around, and bend forward to touch our toes.

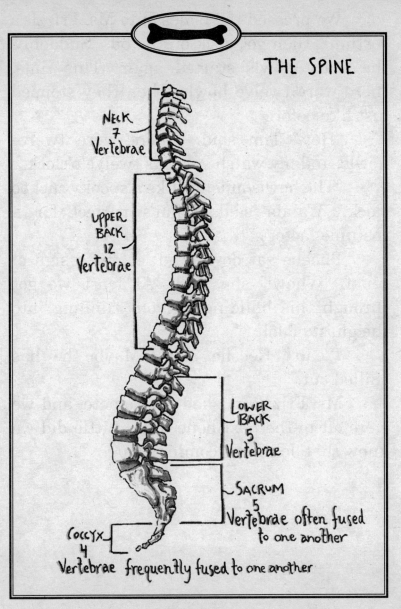

THE SPINE

NECK
7
Vertebrae

UPPER
BACK
12
Vertebrae

LOWER
BACK
5
Vertebrae

SACRUM
5
Vertebrae often fused
to one another

COCCYX
4
Vertebrae frequently fused to one another

We pressed the bones onto Ms. Frizzle's costume, then got back on the bus. Suddenly, the scary howls started again. This time, there were twelve howls. Then they stopped just like before.

"Hey," Tim said. "There were twelve howls, and my watch says it's twelve o'clock."

"The howls must be like a spooky cuckoo clock," Wanda said. "That's perfect for a costume factory."

Phoebe sat down and let out a sigh of relief. "Whew!" she said. "At least we got through this building without running into the ghost of John."

"Yeah," Keesha said. "Maybe he has chilled out."

Ms. Frizzle pushed the remote, and we were off to the next bone hunt. Little did we know that John was coming along.

CHAPTER 6

We were in Stockroom E, and I felt as if we had been in the costume factory all day. But it was only lunchtime. We were hungry, all right, and Ms. Frizzle came to the rescue.

"Get your cheese sandwiches and milk," she called as she opened a cooler that was on the front seat. We all had fruit for dessert.

"Eating the right food is a must for your growing bones," Ms. Frizzle said. "And for my bones, too. Even though my bones aren't getting any longer or larger, they still need the right vitamins and minerals to keep them healthy."

From D.A.'s Notebook
Feed Your Bones!

By the time most people are 16 to 20 years old, their bones have grown to their full size.

But bones are constantly losing calcium and collagen. We can replace these nutrients and help keep bones strong by eating foods that have lots of calcium and Vitamin D.

Milk, cheese, broccoli, and soy beans are good sources of calcium.

Sunshine helps our bodies make Vitamin D, and Vitamin D helps our bodies absorb calcium.

The lunch made us all feel stronger and ready to go on with our bone search. We had to hurry to get back to school in time for our party.

"What bones are in this stockroom, Ms. Frizzle?" I asked.

"There are ribs over here," she answered, pointing to the shelves on one side of the room, "and arms over there," pointing to the opposite wall. "Let's split up into two groups and start the search."

Phoebe, who was missing her ribs, teamed up with Wanda, Tim, and Keesha. They found a rib cage for Phoebe very quickly.

True and False Ribs
by Phoebe

Most people have 12 pairs of ribs. The first 7 are joined at the front by a flat bone called the sternum (or breastbone).

Pairs 8, 9, and 10 are joined in the

---

front to the ribs above. They're called "false ribs."

The bottom pairs, 11 and 12, are called "floating ribs." They are not joined to anything.

Altogether, the bones are known as the rib cage. The ribs protect the heart and lungs, which are safe inside the cage of bones.

THE RIB CAGE

LUNGS

HEART

LIVER

SPLEEN

STOMACH

Carlos still needed his arm bones. Arnold, Ralphie, and I helped him look.

As it turned out, Carlos was the one who found his missing bones. "These arm bones fit me just right," he said.

Each bone went from the shoulder to the forearm, where it fit into the elbow joint.

"Now I have an elbow," Carlos said, "but where is my funny bone?"

Ha! Ha!
by Carlos

Do you know why the arm bone is funny? Because its name is humerus. Humerus sounds the same as humorous. Get it?

"You won't find any real funny bones in these boxes, Carlos," the Friz told him. "The funny bone is actually not a bone at all. It's a spot on your elbow where a nerve runs over the end of the bone. The nerve is just under the surface of the skin — that's why it hurts when you hit your elbow against something."

"Ouch!" I said. Just thinking about it hurt. "There's nothing funny about that."

Phoebe and Carlos looked good in their full skeleton costumes. There were only three of us now with missing parts:

Arnold needed collarbones and shoulder blades.

51

Ralphie needed hands.

And I was looking for my forearms. Then we could get out of that creepy factory!

"According to the map, all these bones should be in the next building," Ms. Frizzle said. "Let's move! Last stop, Stockroom F!"

We got on the bus, and Ms. Frizzle pushed the *start* button on the remote. Nothing happened.

She tried again, but we didn't move an inch.

Then the lights went from dim to pitch-black.

"Uh-oh," Wanda said. "Could this be a power failure — or are we in for another visit from the ghost?"

We looked out the bus windows. That's when we got the biggest skeleton scare of our lives. And it wasn't just the ghost of John. Now there were five or six skeleton ghosts glowing in the dark!

The skeletons were doing a strange dance, bending and twisting, twirling and whirling around. Then suddenly, they just vanished.

The lights turned on again.

"Weird," Tim said.

"Scary," Ralphie said. "Let's vanish ourselves. I want out of here."

Ms. Frizzle tried the remote again. This time, it worked. The bus glided along into the last stockroom.

CHAPTER 7

"This factory sure is a spooky place!" Carlos said.

"Yeah, but I'm beginning to think there's a trick behind those disappearing skeletons," Keesha said.

I thought Keesha might be right.

We were inside Stockroom F, searching through more boxes full of bones. We heard a single howl, so we knew it was already one o'clock. We had to hurry.

Arnold held up two short, thin bones and two wide, flat ones. "I think I've found the bones I need," he said.

Bumpy Bones
by Arnold

Collarbones stick out. You can feel their shape with your fingers. These bumpy bones join the top of the rib cage to the shoulders. Another name for collarbone is clavicle.

Shoulders have two other parts: the end of the humerus bone (the arm bone) and the flat bone at the top of the back, called the shoulder blade, or scapula.

Shoulders do a big job! They hold up the top of your body.

BACK VIEW OF THE SHOULDER

CLAVICLE (collarbone)

SCAPULA (shoulder blade)

HUMERUS (armbone)

I was not having much luck finding my arm bones. Like the lower leg, each forearm has two bones.

Which Arm Bone Is Which?
by D.A.

The bone that is on the same side of the arm as the thumb is called the radius.

The bone on the side opposite the thumb is the ulna.

I found a set of forearms that fit, but one of the bones had a tear in it.

"If that were a real, living bone, it would mend itself," Ms. Frizzle told me. "But we can sew it together later. Everyone to the bus."

Taking Care of Broken Bones
by D.A.

Even though bones are very hard, they can crack or break in a fall or accident.

Cracks and breaks are called fractures.

A broken bone will heal by itself in 3 to 10 weeks, but it needs to be held inplace while it's healing.

First an X ray is taken to find out how bad the fracture is. If it is really bad, the doctor may have to straighten the bone by hand, or even operate. Sometimes a screw or pin has to be put in to hold the pieces of bone together.

> A splint or a cast is put around the healing bone. This helps the bone to grow back in its correct position.

I was excited to have my arm bones, even if one of them was torn. It would be a lot easier to fix than a real broken bone.

"Now we know how a doctor treats a broken bone," Wanda said, "but how does the bone actually heal itself?"

"It's simple, Wanda," Ms. Frizzle answered. "Broken bones heal by growing together again."

The magic monitor showed us what happens.

A Broken Bone Heals

1. The blood around the break hardens and covers the broken ends of bone, like a scab that forms on your skin when you cut yourself.

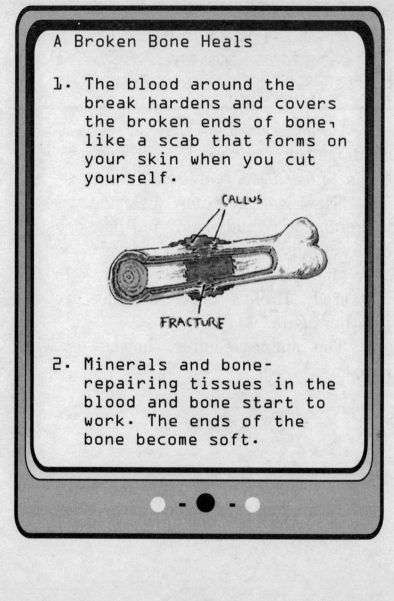

CALLUS

FRACTURE

2. Minerals and bone-repairing tissues in the blood and bone start to work. The ends of the bone become soft.

Then new bone, called callus, starts to grow from the broken ends.

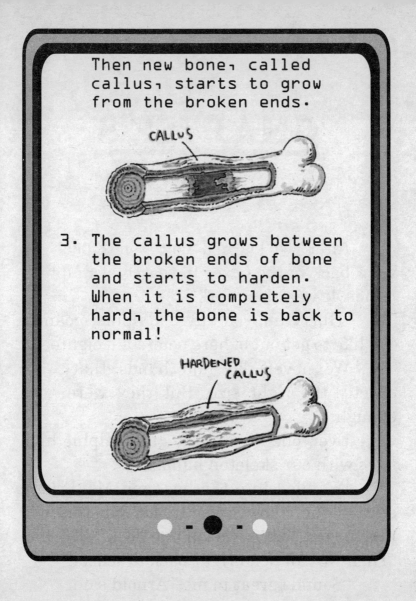

CALLUS

3. The callus grows between the broken ends of bone and starts to harden. When it is completely hard, the bone is back to normal!

HARDENED CALLUS

CHAPTER 8

After we learned how bones heal, we went back to the boxes in search of Ralphie's hands. It was slow work.

"Hurry up, you guys," Ralphie moaned. "I'd like to get out of here before I'm eighteen."

We never did find hands that were exactly the right size. But they were good enough.

Everyone lined up to give Ralphie high fives with our skeleton hands.

We piled into the bus, and Ms. Frizzle started the conveyor belt. "I think this will take us outside to the loading dock," she said. "Then we can head right back to school."

"Sounds great to me," Arnold said.

Handy Hands
by Ralphie

Our hands have many small bones – 27 in each hand, to be exact.

Each finger has three hinge joints, and the thumb can bend toward the fingers. All this helps hands to grip, hold, and pick up even tiny things.

Many of the muscles that move hand bones are in the forearm. If not, hands would be too bulky to do their delicate work.

I tried to look on the bright side. "The costumes are really neat," I said. "And we learned a lot about the human skeleton."

"And it was better than spending the whole day in school," Ralphie whispered.

While we were talking, the bus was gliding along on the conveyor belt. Up ahead we saw a dark tunnel.

"Uh-oh," Arnold said. "I don't like the looks of this. Please stop the bus, Ms. Frizzle!"

Ms. Frizzle pushed the *stop* button on the remote, but it didn't work. It was too late! We were already gliding into the dark tunnel.

"Don't worry," Ms. Frizzle told us. "We'll probably be out of this in a jiffy."

It was hard not to worry when we saw the eerie lights pop up in the dark around us.

The dancing skeletons!

We were ready to duck under the seats when we came out of the tunnel into a lighted room. The conveyor belt stopped.

We were in a workroom, with sewing machines and tables covered with wires, tools, and paints.

A group of people in black bodysuits were waving to us. One by one they pulled off their hooded masks and smiled.

The glowing skeletons weren't the ghost of John and his friends after all!

"The ghosts were *people*?" Ralphie asked. "What's going on here?"

"Well, we *are* in a costume factory,"

Ms. Frizzle said with a smile. "We should have guessed."

One of the skeleton ghosts came over to say hello.

"I'm Sally," she said. "I work here. We hope we didn't scare you *too* much. We needed to try out this new electric costume. When we heard you were at the factory today, we thought this would be a good time for a Halloween trick."

Sally showed us how the suit worked. When she pressed a button, the bones glowed an eerie neon-green color. When she pressed the button again, the light went out, and the suit was completely black again. In a dark room, it would look like the skeleton just disappeared!

"It was a good trick," Wanda said. "Some of us were really scared."

"Not me," said Arnold. "I knew the ghosts weren't real all along."

"ARNOLD!!!" we all said.

He just smiled.

CHAPTER 9

We said good-bye to Sally and the other "ghosts." As we were getting on the bus, we heard a voice calling, "Ms. Frizzle! Ms. Frizzle!"

It was Hugh Mann, the head of the costume company. He was driving a small electric cart piled high with boxes. He stopped the cart and picked up one of the boxes.

"I'm sorry about the mix-up with your costumes, Ms. Frizzle," he said, handing her the box. "Here is something extra for your class."

Ms. Frizzle opened the box. Inside were pull-on skull masks! Now our costumes were *really* complete. There was even a small lizard skull mask for Liz.

"Hey, this is neat!" Tim said. "Thanks, Mr. Mann."

Back in our classroom, we had time for one more lesson. We learned about the bones that make up the skull. This is a very important part of the skeleton since it protects the brain and the organs that let us see, hear, smell, and taste — which are, of course, the eyes, ears, nose, and mouth.

The lower jawbone is the only bone in the skull that we can move. The other bones have fixed joints to hold them in place.

The smallest bone in the body is found in the skull. The stirrup, smaller than a grain of rice, is deep inside the ear.

"The skull looks like one big piece of bone," Ms. Frizzle said. She pointed to the skull on our poster skeleton, Skinny. "But it is actually made up of twenty-two different bones. Fourteen bones make up the face. The other eight form the forehead and the round dome at the back. This part is called the cranium. The cranium is like a bony helmet that protects the brain."

"How come the skull doesn't have a nose — just a hole?" Phoebe asked. "I always wondered about that."

"Your nose may feel like bone," Ms. Frizzle said, "but a big part of it is cartilage covering a bony framework. That's why you can bend the tip of your nose, like you can bend your ears. The outside of your ears is also cartilage."

"The eye sockets in the skull are so big," Wanda said.

"They have to be large to hold eyes that are the size of golf balls," the Friz explained. "Remember, we can see less than half of the eyeball. The rest is behind our eyelids and skin, protected by the bones."

"This skull has teeth," Arnold pointed out. "Teeth aren't bone, are they?"

"No," Ms. Frizzle said, "but they are rooted in the spongy bone that makes up the jaw. And they are covered with enamel, the hardest material in your body. Teeth that don't rot away or get pulled stay in the skull, just like they were part of the bone."

From D.A.'s Notebook
A Skeleton Begins

Your skeleton starts to grow before you are born. At first, it is made of soft, rubbery stuff called cartilage.

By the time you are born, some of the cartilage has begun to harden into bone. As time goes by, more of the soft cartilage slowly gets replaced by bone.

CARTILAGE
(growth plates)

A six-year-old's skeleton is mostly hard bone, but small pads of cartilage remain. These special cartilage pads, called growth plates, allow you to keep on growing for another 10 to 14 years until your bones reach their full length.

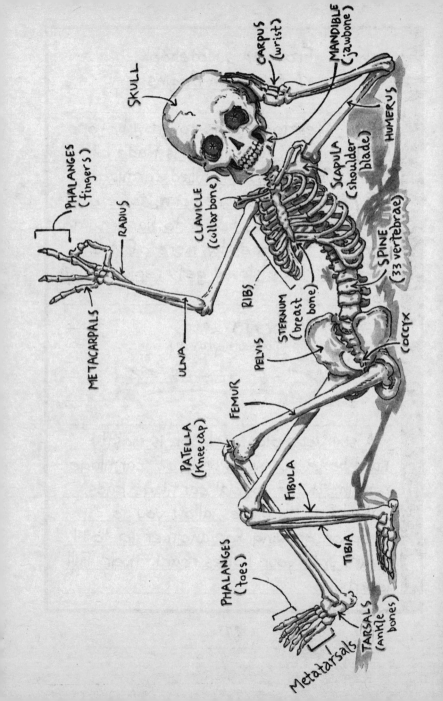

Ms. Frizzle unrolled a huge skeleton poster and spread it on the floor. Then she handed us each a marker.

"Now that we know the parts of the human skeleton, we can finish this poster. Let's write in the name of the bones you found in the costume company. Wanda, you start."

We spent the rest of the day putting labels on the chart.

When our work was done, Ms. Frizzle wheeled in a cart loaded with pumpkin cupcakes, skeleton cookies, and punch. "We had our trick at the factory. Now it's time for a treat," she said. It was the best surprise of the day.

"Now *this* is something a skeleton can get his teeth into!" Carlos said.

"No bones about it," Phoebe added.

It looked like it was going to be a great Halloween after all.

GUESS WHO?
A FRIZ QUIZ

"Do all animals have a skeleton like ours?" Ralphie asked Ms. Frizzle.

"That's a no, Ralphie," Ms. Frizzle said. "The big difference is the backbone. Humans and other animals that have a backbone are called *vertebrates*. (Remember — the bones that make up the backbone are called *vertebrae*.) All other animals — insects, worms, jellyfish, and about a million other kinds — don't have a backbone. They are called *invertebrates*. There are lots more invertebrates in the world than vertebrates."

Ms. Frizzle started handing out a worksheet as she spoke. "Vertebrates live on land and in the water. On these worksheets you will see five skeletons with backbones. Can you name the vertebrate animals by looking at their skeletons?"

Phoebe got all of them right. How about you?

Here's a hint: None of the animals is extinct.

To check your answers, turn to page 76 and turn it upside down.

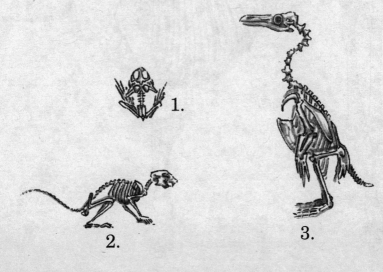

1.

2.

3.

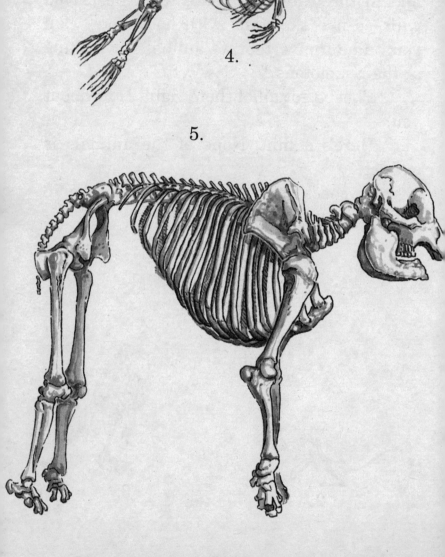

4.

5.

1. Frog 2. Squirrel 3. Penguin 4. Seal 5. Elephant